# While I Wait

# While I Wait

Written by Robin Hasslen

Illustrated by:

Candy Yaghjian Waites

David Yaghjian

Becca Holliday

Savannah Holliday

Clare Yaghjian

Susy Yaghjian

Jessica Hasslen Steyn

ISBN: 978-1-68201-128-7

P★olaris  Publications
*an  Imprint  of*
North  Star  Press

www.northstarpress.com

This book evolved out of the world's period of social distancing during the 2020 Coronavirus Pandemic. It is the product of a family of artists, offspring of Edmund and Dorothy Candy Yaghjian whose creative genes live on. The writing reflects the experience of the youngest family member during the pandemic. Each page is illustrated by a different person and because of social distancing, was gathered online from Canada to Australia with Minnesota and the Carolinas in between. It is shared as an expression of the joy of creativity and family despite external circumstances and is offered in the hope that it conveys the same to its readers.

# A Note to Parents

Changes affecting routines and expectations in the lives of young children can be both confusing and overwhelming. This book is meant to reflect some of those changes as we all navigate new ways of being in the world. As you read this book with your child, discuss any feelings that each page/situation/drawing may evoke. We, the authors have purposefully not given voice to specific feelings so as not to assume that each child's experiences or responses to experiences are the same.

Waiting is hard work.

But sometimes we HAVE to wait.

So let's see how we can
make that waiting FUN!

While I wait
to go out to
the park,

I build a fort in my room.

While I wait to
see my friends
again,

I draw a picture
to send in the mail.

While I wait for my big brother to finish his schoolwork on the computer,

I make hearts to hang in the window.

While I wait to visit Grandma and Grandpa,

I practice wearing my mask.

While I wait for
Mama to come
home from work
at the hospital,
and take a shower,

I build a block tower with Daddy.

While I wait to
go to daycare,

I play school with my toys.

While I wait to go to the library for story hour,

I read my picture books over and over.

While I wait for my abuela and abuelo to come visit,

I talk to them and see them on video.

While I wait to go
to the fair,

I play with Grandpa's cow.

While I wait for Daddy to go to the grocery store,

I try not to get tired of eating
the same thing all the time.

While I wait for Mom and Dad to turn off the news,

I put on a towel and pretend I am a superhero coming to save everyone.

# While we wait,

## we know the whole world waits with us...

And we all hope
for a new kind of
world
with hearts
and superheros
and lots of
singing and
stories,
and of course...
families.

# THE YAGHJIANS

**CANDY YAGHJIAN WAITES** is a former college program director, state and county elected official, and currently president of Seniors on the Move in Columbia, SC.

**ROBIN YAGHJIAN HASSLEN** is a doting Nana and a retired university professor of Early Childhood Education and Development, and currently lives in Zebulon, NC.

**DAVID HENRY YAGHJIAN**, though distracted by various jobs to earn money, has spent most of his life painting in Columbia, SC.

**SUSAN YAGHJIAN** is a high school Science teacher living in Dubbo, NSW, Australia where she has resided since 1995.

**JESSICA HASSLEN STEYN** is the mother of Nadia, who was the inspiration for this book. She works with adolescents living with HIV, and resides in Zebulon, NC.

**REBECCA HOLLIDAY** was born in Maine and now works in disability care in Newcastle, Australia.

**SAVANNAH HOLLIDAY** is a social worker in the public health system in Melbourne, Australia.

**CLARE YAGHJIAN** is currently overseeing the design and operations of an e-sports startup she's building with her partner in Vancouver, BC.

Contact via email: rchasslen@gmail.com